MAJOR EVENTS IN U.S. MILITARY HISTORY

What Happened on D-Day?

Craig Boutland

ROSEN PUBLISHING

Published in 2024 by The Rosen Publishing Group, Inc.
2544 Clinton Street, Buffalo, NY 14224

Portions of this work were originally authored by Charlie Samuels and published as *D-Day*. All new material this edition authored by Craig Boutland.

For Brown Bear Books Ltd:
Children's Publisher: Anne O'Daly
Design Manager: Keith Davis
Picture Manager: Sophie Mortimer

Picture Credits:
Front Cover: U.S. Government: U.S Navy.
Interior: All images Robert Hunt Library.

Cataloging-in-Publication Data

Names: Boutland, Craig.
Title: What happened on D-Day? / Craig Boutland.
Description: New York : Rosen Young Adult, 2024. | Series: Major events in U.S. military history | Includes glossary and index.
Identifiers: ISBN 9781499474428 (pbk.) | ISBN 9781499474435 (library bound) | ISBN 9781499474442 (ebook)
Subjects: LCSH: World War, 1939-1945--Campaigns--France--Normandy--Juvenile literature.
Classification: LCC D756.5.N6 B68 2024 | DDC 940.54'21421--dc23

Manufactured in the United States of America

CPSIA Compliance Information: Batch #CSRYA24. For further information, contact Rosen Publishing, New York, New York, at 1-800-237-9932.

Contents

Introduction 4
German Victories 6
Japan Attacks the United States 10
Strategic Plans 12
The Atlantic Wall 16
Training for D-Day 18
Making the Decision 20
Attack from the Air 22
Onto the Beaches 24
Utah Beach 26
Omaha Beach 30
Germany Strikes Back 34
Success in Normandy 36
Advance to the Rhine 38
Victory in Europe 42
TIMELINE 44
GLOSSARY 46
FURTHER INFORMATION 47
INDEX 48

Introduction

Before dawn on June 6, 1944, the Allies—led by the United States and Britain—launched Operation Overlord, the biggest amphibious attack in history. By nightfall more than 160,000 soldiers would land on five beaches in Normandy in occupied France. Some landings were straightforward. Others faced fierce resistance from the Germans. But everyone knew that if the Allies could at least get a foothold on mainland Europe, D-Day would be a turning point in World War II.

Long-Term Strategy

D-Day had been years in the planning. Before it could take place, the Allies had to defeat the Germans in other theaters, to draw men away from northern France. Hundreds of thousands of Allied troops had to be assembled, along with the ships to transport them, vehicles, gas, weapons, and ammunition. The Allied air forces had to gain air superiority over the German Luftwaffe. Resistance fighters in France had to destroy German communications.

The timing of the operation was in doubt until the last minute. On the evening of June 4, the Allied Supreme Commander, U.S. General Dwight D. Eisenhower, studied the weather forecast and made his decision. D-Day would be June 6, 1944.

British reinforcements land on Sword Beach to support the initial assault groups. The Allied soldiers came ashore in a series of waves.

◀ This view from a landing craft at Omaha Beach shows U.S. troops wading through the surf from their landing craft.

► German motorcycle troops in spring 1940. The Germans used vehicles, tanks, and airplanes to make rapid advances.

German Victories

From mid-1940, Germany controlled the whole coastline of western Europe, stretching from the Spanish border in southern France to the North Cape in Norway. The German armed forces had achieved an astonishing series of victories. Landing an army in Europe involved tough decisions for the United States and Britain.

Before 1939, Nazi Germany had used diplomacy to take over Austria and occupy parts of Czechoslovakia. Adolf Hitler, the German leader, had even greater ambitions. On September 1, 1939, Germany invaded Poland. Two days later, Britain and France declared war on Germany. Two weeks later, the Soviet Union also invaded Poland. Germany and the Soviet Union divided the country between themselves.

The Fall of Europe

After a period of inaction known as the Phony War, the Nazis invaded Denmark and Norway in April 1940. The next month, they invaded France, Luxembourg, Belgium, and the Netherlands.

BLITZKRIEG

"Blitzkrieg" (lightning war) was a tactic developed by the Germans in the early years of World War II. It relied on rapid advances using Panzer tanks, Stuka dive-bombers, and large numbers of infantry. The Germans stormed through the Low Countries and France in 1940. Once a target was selected, it was bombed from the air and then attacked by tanks and infantry. As the infantry mopped up any remaining resistance, the dive-bombers and Panzers moved straight on to the next target.

◀ German Stuka dive-bombers fly in formation to support ground operations. They attacked their targets in a near-vertical dive.

▲ German tanks parade in front of the Arc de Triomphe in Paris after the fall of the French capital in May 1940.

The British army, which had been sent to protect France, was defeated. It had to be rescued from the beaches of Dunkirk.

Britain Fights On

Britain stood alone. The German air force, the Luftwaffe, bombed British cities, and German submarines (U-boats) attacked convoys carrying supplies across the Atlantic. Hitler planned to invade Britain but was unable to destroy the Royal Air Force (RAF). In fall 1940, he decided to plan the invasion of his former ally, the Soviet Union. The same month, Germany, Italy, and Japan formed an alliance, known as the Axis. Italy invaded Greece the same year, and, using bases in its colony of Libya, attacked the British stronghold of Egypt in North Africa.

Operation Barbarossa

In early 1941, German troops arrived in North Africa, where their Italian allies were fighting the British. In spring German armies took over Yugoslavia and helped the Italians to conquer Greece. Finally, in June 1941, three million German troops invaded the Soviet Union in what was code-named Operation Barbarossa.

President Franklin Roosevelt made it clear he would help Britain but was reluctant to declare war. Instead, he gave aid to Britain by providing supplies under the Lend-Lease program.

BRITAIN STANDS ALONE

In July 1940, Hitler planned to destroy the RAF and then invade Britain across the English Channel. In the Battle of Britain, the Luftwaffe attacked the RAF and its bases for two months. When the RAF survived, the Luftwaffe started the "Blitz." From September 7, 1940, until May 21, 1941, German bombers repeatedly attacked British cities. London suffered most. It was bombed for 57 consecutive nights. Of the 40,000 civilians who died in the Blitz, half were Londoners.

◄ Firefighters try to save burning buildings during the Blitz, the sustained German bombing campaign against London.

Japan Attacks the United States

On December 7, 1941, Japan launched a surprise attack on the U.S. Pacific Fleet based in Pearl Harbor. U.S. President Franklin D. Roosevelt called this "a day that will live in infamy." The United States was now at war.

▼ A rescue boat approaches burning U.S. warships on "Battleship Row" after the Japanese attack on Pearl Harbor in Hawaii.

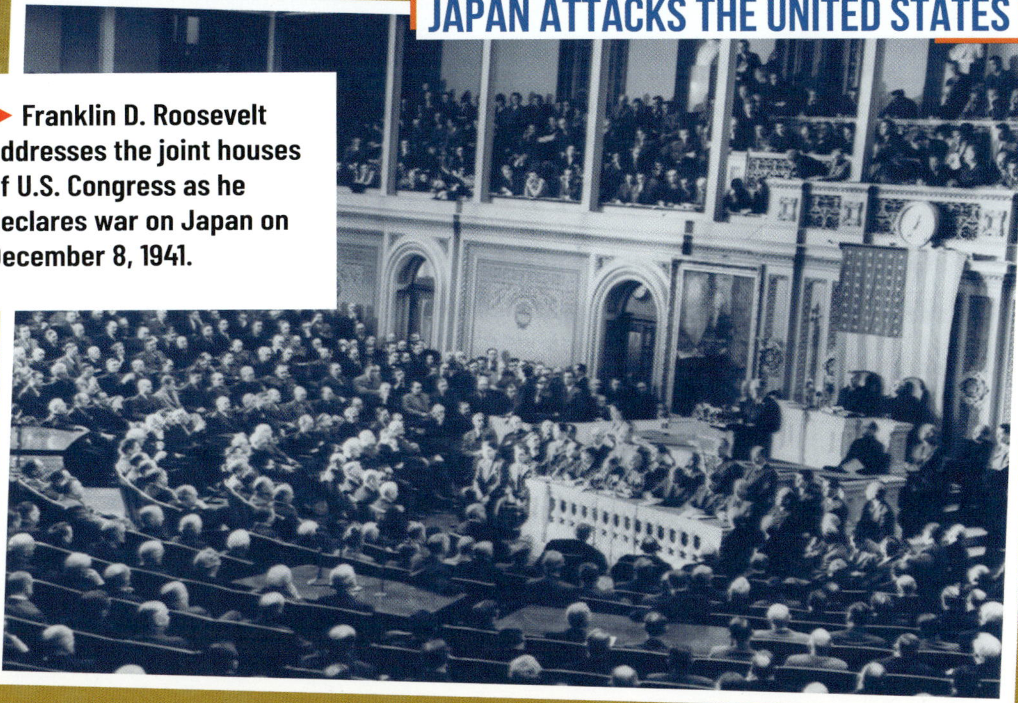

▶ Franklin D. Roosevelt addresses the joint houses of U.S. Congress as he declares war on Japan on December 8, 1941.

On a Sunday morning, around 360 warplanes of the Imperial Japanese Navy attacked the U.S. naval base in Pearl Harbor, Hawaii. The surprise strike was intended to stop the U.S. Navy interfering in Japan's planned attacks on British and Dutch territories in Southeast Asia.

At War

More than 2,300 Americans died in the attacks, and the Pacific Fleet was crippled. The next day, Congress declared war on Japan. As Japan and Germany were allies, Hitler declared war on the United States four days later. The United States was at war in both Asia and Europe.

WAR LEADER

In 1940, the Democrat Franklin Delano Roosevelt won an unprecedented third term as U.S. president. At the start of the war, he supported the British by supplying them with arms. After the attack on Pearl Harbor, he was central in the alliance fighting the Axis powers. He also planned for postwar life, including the setting up of the United Nations to settle international disputes. He died on April 12, 1945, a month before Germany surrendered.

Strategic Plans

▲ A British soldier captures a German tank and its crew during the Battle of El Alamein in the Egyptian desert.

Victories late in 1942 gave the Allies the upper hand in the war. There were intense discussions between them, however, about the best way forward. The United States had to decide whether it would concentrate its resources against Germany or Japan. Britain wanted the major effort to be in the Mediterranean. Joseph Stalin wanted the western Allies to invade western Europe as soon as possible.

At the start of 1942, Winston Churchill and Franklin D. Roosevelt met at a conference codenamed Arcadia in Washington, DC. They decided to defeat Germany first before defeating Japan. Eventually that meant Allied armies would have to invade Europe.

North Africa

At a second Washington conference in June 1942, Roosevelt and Churchill agreed to open a second front in North Africa. Capturing North Africa would open a possible route into southern Europe via the Italian island of Sicily.

TEHRAN CONFERENCE

In December 1943, Roosevelt and Churchill met Soviet leader Joseph Stalin in Tehran in Iran to discuss how best for the Allies to defeat Germany. Stalin pressed the other leaders to launch their invasion of western Europe as soon as possible. He wanted the invasion to divert German resources from the Eastern Front, where the Red Army was heavily engaged against the major part of the German army.

▲ The Allied leaders are seated in Tehran in 1943: Churchill (right), Roosevelt (center) and Joseph Stalin (left).

Turning Point in the Desert

In North Africa, Field Marshal Erwin Rommel was leading his Afrika Korps east toward the Suez Canal, Britain's route to its colony in India. At El Alamein, in the Egyptian desert, the British first stopped Rommel and then forced him to retreat. It was the Allies' first major victory over the Germans.

At the same time, U.S. forces landed in Morocco and Algeria in a set of surprise landings code-named Operation Torch, trapping the German and Italian forces in North Africa. Victory in North Africa was

Massive Allied LST (Landing Ship, Tank) are shown at Anzio in Italy. Such assault vessels were needed for D-Day.

German soldiers retreat through the snow after the defeat at Stalingrad. The battle was the turning point on the Eastern Front.

followed by an invasion of Sicily in July 1943. After the island fell, they landed on the "toe" of Italy in September. To get around German defensive lines, the Allies made another landing on the coast at Anzio in January 1944.

Useful Practice

By January 1944, the western Allies had decided to invade France as the next step toward defeating Germany. The series of earlier landings had shown the Allies how to coordinate large amphibious operations. They learned about using air, naval, and land forces together. The lessons would be vital when it came to invading France on D-Day.

STALINGRAD

Allied victories in 1943 did not only come in North Africa and Italy. The German 6th Army had besieged the Soviet city of Stalingrad since August 1942. During the bitter winter, a Soviet counterattack trapped the Germans inside the city. After desperate fighting in the ruined city, the whole army surrendered. The defeat was a turning point of the whole war. The Germans began to retreat while the Soviet Red Army pursued them toward Germany itself.

The Atlantic Wall

In 1944, the Germans knew that the United States and Britain would invade northern Europe. They built huge defenses along the French, Belgian, and Dutch coasts facing the English Channel. These defenses were known as the Atlantic Wall.

▲ German troops march past the gigantic fortifications of the Atlantic Wall in France in April 1944, just two months before D-Day.

The Germans placed huge guns along the coast of the Pas-de-Calais region, where Hitler believed the Allies would attempt to land.

In January 1944, Field Marshal Erwin Rommel took charge of the defenses and ordered them to be strengthened. Concrete gun emplacements were built along the coast. Barbed wire and other obstacles were piled on the beaches. Millions of mines were laid at sea.

Where Will They Land?

The problem for the Germans was which part of the channel to concentrate on. Hitler believed the Allies would target the Pas-de-Calais region, near the northern French border with Belgium. His commanders were not so sure.

ERWIN ROMMEL

Rommel had served as a Panzer commander during the fall of France and had led the Afrika Korps in North Africa. Hitler made Rommel a field marshal and asked him to reinforce the defenses along the French coast. Rommel disagreed with his superiors about the best way to prevent an invasion. The disagreement meant the Normandy coastal defenses were weaker than they should have been. Implicated in a plot to kill Hitler, Rommel committed suicide in 1944.

▲ U.S. soldiers exercise on a quayside during the buildup to D-Day. Some 75,000 U.S. troops arrived in Britain ready for the landings.

Training for D-Day

In May 1943, British and U.S. planners agreed to land an army in northern Europe within a year. D-Day itself was planned for May 1944. U.S. industry geared up to manufacture the huge amount of military hardware needed for the invasion. At the same time, American troops crossed the Atlantic to assemble in Britain.

From 1943, hundreds of thousands of U.S. troops arrived in Britain. Beaches in southern England were similar to those in France, so they were used to practice amphibious landings. Civilians were banned from the coast to keep the preparations secret. However, although thousands of ships and landing craft were requisitioned for use, there were still not enough by May 1944. The landings were put back one month.

Deceiving Hitler

As the invasion came closer, the Allies carried out a deception exercise. They managed to convince the Germans that the invasion would come near Calais. The deception was easier because Hitler already expected the invasion to come there.

TRAGIC REHEARSAL

In April and May 1944, the Allies carried out full-scale live-fire invasion rehearsals at Slapton Sands in Devon on the English coast. One rehearsal, Operation Tiger, turned into a tragedy when German E-boats attacked the landing craft. The attack was made worse by poor Allied command and communications. In all, 946 U.S. servicemen died. Since the rehearsals were carried out in great secrecy, the disaster was quietly forgotten. The full story only became known after the end of the war.

▶ Hundreds of Allied tanks and other vehicles are stockpiled ready to be deployed during the invasion of France.

Making the Decision

The invasion of Europe was code-named Operation Overlord. Months of preparation went into getting the Allied forces ready. However, the tides and the weather had to be just right for Overlord to start. Allied overall commander General Dwight D. Eisenhower had the responsibility of making the final decision.

SHAEF (Supreme Headquarters Allied Expeditionary Force) planned D-Day under the command of Eisenhower (front, center).

There were only three days each month when high tides in Normandy would give troops time to get ashore. Winds needed to be light so that landing craft were not swamped in the surf. Cloud cover could be no more than 60 percent so bombers could see their targets.

A Final Delay

Eisenhower got a long-range weather forecast and ordered preparations to begin on May 29. By June 3 the weather had gotten so bad that he ordered a 24-hour delay. Then the U.S. Army meteorologist predicted there would be a 24-hour window of better weather from the afternoon of June 5. Eisenhower consulted his senior generals and made the decision to go ahead. June 6 would be D-Day.

FRENCH RESISTANCE

On the evening of June 5, 1944, the BBC in London broadcast a line from a poem by the French poet Paul Verlaine. This was a secret message to the French Resistance that the Allied invasion would begin within 48 hours and that they should start sabotage raids against the Germans. The Resistance carried out hundreds of sabotage operations against power lines, transportation hubs, and communications networks to isolate the Germans in Normandy before the landings got underway.

▶ French Resistance fighters prepare for the sabotage campaign against the Germans after hearing secret messages from the BBC.

Dozens of Allied gliders lie abandoned in fields behind the beaches. Many gliders crashed on landing.

Attack from the Air

Thousands of troops moved into their transport to cross the English Channel on June 5, 1944. Most were in ships and landing craft, but just under 20,000 took to the air, to guard the flanks of the sea-borne invasion and to sow disruption in rear areas. These men were the first Allied troops to land in France on June 6.

▲ Paratroopers of the 101st Airborne Division board their airplane in England on June 5 ready to jump over France.

In the early hours of June 6, 13,000 Allied troops parachuted into Normandy. Another 4,000 landed in 500 gliders. The U.S. 82nd and 101st Airborne Divisions landed behind Utah Beach to block routes for German reinforcements.

The Plan Goes Wrong

Under heavy fire from German defenders, many pilots dropped their men far from the planned landing zones. Scattered across the countryside, the paratroopers took time to organize themselves. Many staggered around looking for their comrades and skirmishing with the enemy.

SCREAMING EAGLES

Formed at the end of World War I, the 101st Airborne—nicknamed the "Screaming Eagles"—were a parachute and glider regiment trained for air-assault operations. The 101st Airborne played a major role on D-Day, even though they missed many of their landing zones. Later in the war, they played a prominent role in the Battle of the Bulge around Bastogne, in Belgium.

Onto the Beaches

While the paratroopers and glider-borne forces landed in France, a fleet of ships crossed the English Channel. There were almost 7,000 vessels, from small landing craft to enormous battleships. This was the biggest naval force ever assembled, in what was code-named Operation Neptune.

▲ Allied ships head for France across the English Channel. Each has a barrage balloon overhead to discourage German air attack.

The Allies used destroyers, antisubmarine air patrols, and minefields to seal off the eastern and western approaches to the channel. Meanwhile the invasion vessels assembled and sailed toward Normandy through a route that had been swept clear of enemy mines.

A Safe Passage

Off the French coast, the fleet split into two task forces. Warships bombarded German positions on the coast while five groups of assault craft formed up for the final push to the beaches. Meticulous planning had got the ships to the right position at the right time.

THE FUNNIES

The larger landing craft carried the "Funnies." These specialized British tanks got their name from their odd attachments. Some carried folding box-girder bridges. Others were fitted with rotating chains to smash through minefields. The Funnies included the amphibious Duplex Drive (DD) Sherman tank. It had twin propellers and a waterproof screen around the hull. It could sail ashore and then drive on land on its caterpillar tracks.

▼ U.S. landing craft and amphibious vehicles carry supplies toward the beaches just hours after the first assault waves.

Utah Beach

▲ U.S. troops wade through the surf on their way to Utah Beach. The landings met only light resistance from the Germans.

The area of coast code-named Utah Beach was the farthest west of the landing areas. If troops could get ashore there, they would threaten the important port of Cherbourg. Taking Cherbourg would give the Allies a base from which to land supplies and more men. The landings at Utah were the most successful of D-Day.

The naval and air bombardment had cleared many enemy minefields on the beach, although it had caused little damage to German enemy positions. The main obstacles facing the Allies were not the beach defenses but flooded terrain blocking the way inland.

Lucky Break

As the first landing craft approached Utah at 6:30 a.m., strong currents swept them south. They hit the shore 2,000 yards (1,830 m) from their planned landing zone. Luckily for the U.S. infantrymen, the beach there was more lightly defended than the original zone.

AIR COVER

During the build-up to D-Day, the Allies had attacked many German airfields. That left the Luftwaffe severely disadvantaged as British Spitfires and U.S. Lightnings and Mustangs patrolled the skies. Spitfires flew cover and U.S. Thunderbolts and British Typhoon fighter-bombers attacked German targets and reinforcements on the ground. They tried to destroy German aircraft before they had chance to take off. Only two German airplanes reached the beaches on D-Day.

◀ Bombs from a B-25 Mitchell bomber detonate at a steelworks during the Allied campaign to capture the town of Caen in Normandy.

An Allied rocket ship fires a barrage of high-explosive shells onto German positions to support the landings on Utah Beach.

On seeing the situation, Brigadier General Theodore Roosevelt Jr., son of former President Theodore Roosevelt, quickly decided to make this beach the new location of the landing site. Roosevelt was the only U.S. general to land on D-Day itself.

A Wise Decision

Roosevelt's decision paid off. Not only was the beach less heavily defended. The waters were also calmer. That helped 28 out of the 32 amphibious tanks make it ashore. In any event, they were not really needed. In less than an hour Roosevelt's men had cleared the beach of Germans.

By 9.30 a.m. men and equipment were moving inland. Before noon, the U.S. 4th Division had even made contact with the airborne forces that had landed behind the beach earlier in the day.

A Good Day

By nightfall the men from Utah Beach had moved 4 miles (6.4 km) inland. They had suffered only 200 casualties. Utah was a major success: partly because of the thorough planning, partly luck, and partly Roosevelt's decision to change the landing site.

REPORTERS

News of D-Day traveled fast. Many war reporters and photographers sailed with the invasion forces to report firsthand on the day's action. Their reports and images filled the front pages. The U.S. author Ernest Hemingway landed on Omaha Beach with the seventh wave. Hemingway's wife, Martha Gellhorn, and the veteran reporter Virginia Cowles also reported from the front line. Photographer Robert Capa captured iconic images of U.S. soldiers wading ashore under fire on Omaha Beach.

▼ Among the reporters who landed on D-Day were the author Ernest Hemingway (right) and the photographer Robert Capa (left).

Omaha Beach

Unlike at Utah beach, the U.S. landings at Omaha Beach met heavy resistance. The naval bombardment had barely affected the German defenses. As the landing craft carrying the infantrymen approached the beach, the German guns opened fire. Many U.S. soldiers were killed before they could reach dry land.

U.S. assault troops huddle behind the ramp of their landing craft. Ahead of them, disaster is already unfolding on the beach.

U.S. Army Rangers use ropes and tubular ladders to scale the cliff at Pointe du Hoc, just west of the Omaha beachhead.

The 1st and 29th Infantry Divisions landed on a wide sandy beach overlooked by tall cliffs. It was an obvious landing point for an invasion, so the Germans had defended it well, with huge gun emplacements on the cliffs.

Disaster

Enemy guns were not the only problems. The sea was rough and a dozen landing craft sank. Others were pulled off course. Most of the amphibious tanks intended to clear the beach also sank. The air and sea bombardment had missed the beach completely.

POINTE DU HOC

The 2nd Rangers Battalion had the task of destroying a German gun emplacement on Pointe du Hoc, a cliff overlooking the beach. Using grapple hooks and tubular ladders, they scaled the cliff in just 15 minutes, but found the guns had been removed. Eventually a Ranger patrol found five of them in an orchard 1 mile (1.6 km) away and destroyed them. The action is one of the most famous in U.S. Army Ranger history.

▲ Wounded men from 3rd Battalion, 16th Infantry Regiment, shelter from enemy fire under the cliffs at Omaha Beach.

At 6:30 a.m., as the first craft opened their ramps, the German defenders opened fire. Many troops were killed on the landing craft or drowned when they jumped into deep water. Those who got ashore were shell-shocked and missing their equipment. After two hours, not one man had made it off the beach.

Moving Off the Beach

Organization was slowly restored. Small groups of men began to advance. Colonel George Taylor, commander of the 16th Infantry, told the soldiers with him, "There are two kinds of people on this beach: the dead and those about to die." He ordered his men to get moving. By late morning, the first soldiers were starting to fight their way off the beach. Navy destroyers moved close to the shore so that they could shell the German positions.

Breaking Out

By late afternoon, American troops had pushed over a mile (1.6 km) inland. They were far short of their objectives, however. Omaha had suffered the largest loss of life of all the beaches. One out of every 19 men who landed was either dead or wounded.

LEAVING THE BEACH

The Americans hoped to move large numbers of troops off Omaha. Instead, the breakthrough was achieved by small groups of men who improvised their tactics. They cut paths through barbed wire and minefields, and knocked out strongpoints at close range as they inched up the cliffs. By the end of the day, U.S. troops had two isolated footholds that enabled troops to leave the beach. They were enough to let the Americans exploit the weaker German defenses farther inland.

◀ In this famous image of D-Day, soldiers of the U.S. 2nd Infantry Division make their way inland after Omaha Beach has been cleared.

Germany Strikes Back

While American forces landed on Utah and Omaha Beaches, British and Canadian troops landed on three other beaches, code-named Sword, Juno, and Gold. The landings on June 6 had generally gone well, but the next few weeks saw heavy fighting against the German army.

▼ Most German tanks in Normandy at the time of D-Day were Panzer Mk IVs, which were a formidable foe for the Allied tanks.

The landings took the Germans by surprise. Hitler's tank reserves were positioned to face an invasion near Calais. Resistance sabotage slowed German communications, so reserves were slow to arrive.

Heavy Resistance

The Germans already in Normandy fought strongly, however. The Allies suffered heavy casualties as they pushed inland. The U.S. push to the port at Cherbourg faced heavy German resistance. The Allies had planned to seize the town of Caen on D-Day. Instead, it took weeks of hard fighting before they were able to capture Caen.

THE GERMAN PANZERS

When the German tank reserves finally reached Normandy, they were very effective. The German Panzers were superior to Allied tanks in firepower and armor. Allied shells often bounced off German Panthers and Tigers, but a hit from a Panzer on an Allied Sherman, Churchill, or Cromwell tank was usually fatal. In a battle at Villers-Bocage on June 13, a German Tiger commanded by Michael Wittmann single-handedly destroyed 11 Allied tanks and 15 other vehicles.

◀ This German gun position is well camouflaged because the Allies' control of the skies made such positions vulnerable to air attack.

Success in Normandy

The fighting in France during the weeks after D-Day proved difficult for the Allies. The Normandy landscape of small fields separated by deep lanes and thick hedgerows was better for defense than attack. The Germans put up strong resistance around the city of Caen.

Weeks of heavy fighting left the town of Caen in ruins. Caen was the center of transportation routes on the Normandy peninsula.

On the lookout for enemy snipers, U.S. soldiers move carefully along a lane in the Bocage area of Normandy.

The Allies began an operation code-named Cobra. The British and Canadians would attack directly toward Caen while the Americans advanced from the west to encircle the German defenders in the city.

Operation Cobra

On July 25, an air bombardment began the attack. The Allies made quick progress and defeated a German counterattack on August 7. The U.S. advance swung toward Caen, but the Germans escaped the trap. They suffered many casualties, however, and lost much of their equipment. On August 16, Hitler ordered a withdrawal from Normandy.

BOCAGE COUNTRY

Much of the fighting in Normandy took place in a landscape of tiny fields known as the Bocage. This maze of thick hedgerows, tiny roads, and banks of earth up to 10 feet (3 m) high was excellent defensive terrain for the Germans. They fought for every field. The Allies fitted tanks with steel blades to crash through the undergrowth, but the fighting was slow and casualties were high. It took several weeks of heavy fighting before the Allies finally fought their way out of the Bocage.

British paratroopers take cover during the airborne assault on Arnhem in the Netherlands during "Operation Market Garden."

Advance to the Rhine

After breaking out from Normandy, the Allies advanced rapidly northward. They took the French capital, Paris, and pushed into Belgium. However, the German forces did not crumble. Their resistance stiffened as Allied supply problems made further progress difficult.

The Allies freed Paris August 25. After the slow progress through Normandy, Allied troops now sped through northern France, meeting little opposition. By the end of August, two million Allied soldiers were in France.

By early September, the Allies had captured Brussels and Antwerp in Belgium, while Allied troops also landed in the south of France and moved north.

Advance Halted

Allied victory seemed just days away. The advance soon stalled, however, as the Germans regrouped. In the north, the British failure to secure the area around Antwerp meant they did not control a major port. Instead, supplies had to be landed at the D-Day beaches and driven along roads overland, slowing the Allied advance.

MARKET GARDEN

In September 1944, the Allies devised a daring plan to clear a route through the occupied Netherlands into Germany. Paratroops were to seize a line of river and canal crossings, including the bridge over the Rhine River at Arnhem. Allied armor would then speed along this route to capture the important German industrial area of the Ruhr. However, opposition from German armor meant Allied ground forces failed to reach the airborne troops at Arnhem. Operation Market Garden had failed.

▼ British paratroopers are taken prisoner at the end of Market Garden, after Allied armor failed to advance to relieve them.

▲ Soldiers from the U.S. Seventh Army leave their assault craft under enemy fire as they cross the Rhine on March 26, 1944.

Further south, the Allies set foot on German soil for the first time on September 11, but were soon pushed back. Even farther to the south, the advance of the U.S. Third Army was halted when it ran out of fuel.

Toward Germany

During the fall, the Allies marched across France and the Low Countries in heavy rain. They finally captured the Scheldt estuary, which allowed them to use the port at Antwerp. Now they could begin to amass the huge supplies needed for an invasion of Germany. Although the Allies were close to the German border along a front that stretched from Belgium almost to Switzerland, it was becoming clear that the Germans were not about to surrender.

The Battle of the Bulge

The Allies launched advances toward the Ruhr in the north and Frankfurt in the south. But on December 16, the Germans began a shock attack through the dense Ardennes forest between the Allied fronts. The Germans pushed 60 miles (96 km) through Allied lines before finally losing the Battle of the Bulge before Christmas. The Ardennes offensive was Germany's last chance. With Russian troops attacking Germany from the east, the Allies in the west were ready to cross the Rhine into Germany in March 1945.

BRIDGE AT REMAGEN

Adolf Hitler had ordered all bridges across the Rhine to be destroyed to stop the Allied advance. At Remagen, however, troops of the U.S. First Army arrived as German engineers were preparing to blow up a railroad bridge on March 7, 1945. They seized the bridge and used it to secure a toehold on the opposite bank. The Germans desperately tried to destroy the bridge, but it was not until ten days later that it collapsed into the river, having been weakened during the fighting.

▼ A U.S. soldier looks over the bridge at Remagen. Crossing the Rhine was a logistical problem for the Allies, rather than a military one.

Victory in Europe

German armies continued to fight on in 1945 although their cause was hopeless. The western Allies finally crossed the Rhine in force on March 24 and pushed into the heart of Germany. At the same time, the Red Army attacked Berlin from the east. The war in Europe ended in May.

▼ A Red Army soldier waves a Soviet flag over the Chancellery in Berlin after the Russian capture of the city on May 7, 1945.

In mid-April, the western Allies surrounded and captured German Army Group B. The Allies crossed Germany and met up with the Russians on April 24 at Torgau on the Elbe River. But Eisenhower now halted the advance. The Allied leaders had agreed that the Soviet Red Army alone would have the task of taking Berlin.

Boy Soldiers

The Germans were so short of troops that boys as young as 10 and 11 were pressed into service. In April 1945, some 5,000 boys joined the fight against the Red Army in Berlin. Adolf Hitler committed suicide on April 30 while the battle raged in the city's streets. On May 7, 1945, Germany finally surrendered. Nazi rule was over.

DEATH OF HITLER

Adolf Hitler spent his last months in an air-raid shelter near the Chancellery in Berlin. From his bunker, he conducted a desperate bid to stop the Allied advances. Eventually, he realized that defeat was inevitable. On April 29, he married his long-term girlfriend, Eva Braun. The next day, Hitler shot himself and Braun took poison. His bodyguards then burned the bodies.

In the last photograph ever taken of Adolf Hitler, the German leader hands out medals to young soldiers in Berlin in April 1945.

Timeline

1939 September 1: German troops invade Poland, beginning World War II.

1940 May 10: German forces invade Belgium, the Netherlands, and Luxembourg, beginning an offensive on the Western Front.

June 22: France surrenders to Germany.

July–August: In the Battle of Britain, the German Luftwaffe fail to defeat the RAF to open the way for an invasion of Britain.

September 7: German bombers begin the nightly raids on British cities known as the Blitz.

1941 February: German troops arrive in North Africa to help their Italian allies fight the British.

June 22: Hitler launches Operation Barbarossa, when more than 3 million troops invade the Soviet Union.

December 7: Japanese aircraft bomb the U.S. naval base at Pearl Harbor in Hawaii.

December 8: The United States declares war on Japan.

December 12: Adolf Hitler declares war on the United States.

1942 January: President Roosevelt and British Prime Minister Winston Churchill agree to defeat Germany before tackling Japan. Plans for an Allied landing in northern Europe begin.

October: In North Africa, British troops defeat the Germans for the first time at the Battle of El Alamein.

November 8: U.S. troops arrive in North Africa.

1943 February 2: A Soviet counteroffensive lifts the siege of Stalingrad, turning the tide of the war on the Eastern Front.

July 10: British and U.S. troops invade Sicily.

September 3: Allied troops invade mainland Italy.

1944 January 22: U.S. troops stage a large-scale amphibious landing at Anzio in Italy.

April: Full-scale rehearsals for D-Day begin on the southern coast of Britain.

June 4: The Allied Supreme Commander, General Dwight D. Eisenhower, confirms D-Day as June 6.

June 5: The BBC broadcasts secret messages telling the French Resistance to begin a sabotage campaign against German communications.

June 6: D-Day. Thousands of Allied paratroopers and glider troops land in Normandy before dawn. From around 6:30 a.m., thousands more troops land on five beaches. By nightfall, some 160,000 Allied troops have come ashore.

July 25: After weeks of fighting, the Allies begin Operation Cobra, the breakout from Normandy.

August 25: Allied troops liberate Paris.

September: Operation Market Garden, an Allied thrust into the Netherlands, fails to break through to Germany.

December 16: A German attack through the Ardennes begins the Battle of the Bulge, but the Germans are defeated before Christmas.

1945 March 7: U.S. soldiers seize an intact bridge across the Rhine at Remagen.

March 24: U.S. troops cross the Rhinc.

April 24: Allied troops meet Soviet troops advancing from the east at the Elbe River, where the Allied advance halts.

April 30: With Red Army troops fighting in the streets of Berlin, Adolf Hitler commits suicide in his bunker.

May 7: Germany surrenders, ending World War II in Europe.

Glossary

air superiority A situation in which one air force makes it too dangerous for enemy planes to fly.

amphibious An operation that takes place on land and at sea.

armor Armored vehicles, such as tanks or personnel carriers.

Axis The name given to the alliance of Germany, Italy, and Japan.

BBC British Broadcasting Corporation, the national TV and radio station in Britain.

gliders Aircraft without engines that fly by using thermal currents in the air.

infantry Soldiers who are trained and armed to fight on foot.

landing craft Flat-bottomed boats with ramps used to carry troops and equipment onto beaches.

Lend-Lease A U.S. government program that allowed its allies to buy war equipment on credit.

mines Bombs laid at sea or buried in the ground that explode when something touches them.

Panzer The German name for a tank.

paratroopers Soldiers who are trained to parachute into action.

requisitioned Describes something that is temporarily taken over for military use.

Resistance A French organization set up to fight German occupation through acts such as sabotage.

sabotage Destroying equipment and transportation networks to disrupt enemy operations.

stockpile To gather together stores for an operation.

strategic Something that is related to an overall conflict, rather than to a short-term victory in a battle.

theater A major region in which a distinct part of a war is fought.

Further Information

Book

Doeden, Matthew. *D-Day Invasion (Heroes of World War II)*. Lerner Publishing, 2018.

Drez, Ronald J. *D-Day: The Plan, the Invasion, Survivor Stories*. National Geographic, 2015.

Hopkinson, Deborah. *D-Day: The World War II Invasion That Changed History*. Scholastic, 2020.

Rose, Sarah. *D-Day Girls: The Spies Who Armed the Resistance, Sabotaged the Nazis, and Helped Win World War II*. Crown, 2020.

Roscoe, Kelly. *Dwight D. Eisenhower*. Rosen Publishing, 2017.

Tarshis, Laura. *I Survived the Battle of D-Day, 1944*. Scholastic, 2019.

Websites

https://www.army.mil/d-day/history.html
U.S. Army site on D-Day including much visual material and brief accounts of individuals who took part.

https://www.dday-overlord.com/en/
Includes many firsthand accounts from veterans.

https://www.eisenhowerlibrary.gov/research/online-documents/world-war-ii-d-day-invasion-normandy
Details and documents on the decisions made by commander in chief, Dwight D. Eisenhower.

Index

Page numbers in italics refer to illustrations or their captions.

air cover 27
air landings 22–23
Airborne, U.S. 23, *23*
amphibious landings 15, 19
Antwerp 39, 40
Anzio 14, 15
Arcadia conference 13
Ardennes 41
Arnhem 38, 39, *39*
Atlantic Wall 16–17

Battle of Berlin 43
Battle of Britain 9
Battle of El Alamein 12
Battle of the Bulge 41
BBC 21
Belgium 39
Blitz 9, *9*
blitzkrieg ("lightning war") 6, 7
Bocage 37, *37*
Braun, Eva 43
breakout, Allied 36–37
Britain 6, 8, 9, 10

Caen 27, 35, 36, *36*, 37
Calais 17, 19, 35
Capa, Robert 29
casualties 32, 33
Channel crossing 24–25
Cherbourg 26, 35
Churchill, Winston 9, 13, 14
conferences, Allied 13
counterattack, German 34–35

D-Day, date of 20–21
deception exercises 19
defenses, German 16–17
Dunkirk 8

Eastern Front 15
Eisenhower, Dwight D. 20–21, 43
El Alamein 14
Elbe River 43
English Channel, defenses 16–17
Europe, German campaigns in 6–9

France, fall of 7
"Funnies" 25

Gellhorn, Martha 29
"Germany first" strategy 13
Germany, invasion 40–41
gliders 22, 23
Gold Beach 34

hardware 18–19
Hemingway, Ernest 29
Hitler, Adolf 7, 9, 37, 43, *43*

Japan 10
Juno Beach 34

landing craft 25, *25*
landings, D-Day 26–29, 30–33, 34
Luftwaffe 8

Netherlands 38, 39
Normandy 21, 36–37
North Africa 9, *12*, 13–14, 17

Omaha Beach 30–33
Operation Barbarossa 9
Operation Cobra 37
Operation Market Garden 38, 39
Operation Tiger 19

Panzers 35
paratroopers 23
Paris 8, 38, 39
Pas-de-Calais 17
Pearl Harbor 10–11
Phony War 7
Pointe du Hoc 31, *31*
Poland 7

Rangers, U.S. Army 31, *31*
Red Army 42, 43
Remagen 41, *41*
reporters 29, *29*
Resistance, French 21, *21*, 35
Rhine 39, *40*, 41, 42
Rommel, Erwin 14, 17
Roosevelt, Franklin D. 10, 11, 13
Roosevelt, General Theodore Jr. 28

sabotage 21, 35
shipping 24–25
Sicily 15
Slapton Sands 19
Soviet Union 7, 8
Stalin, Joseph 12, 13
Stalingrad 15, *15*
strategy, Allied 12–15, 18–19
Stukas 7
surrender, German 43
Sword Beach 34

tanks 25, 28
task forces 25
Taylor, Colonel George 32
Tehran conference 13, *13*

United States 6, 9, 10–11, 12
Utah Beach 26–29

victory, Allied 42–43

weather forecasts 20–21
Wittmann, Michael 35